MW00808005

HERE
COMES THE
APRIL FOOL!

Dr. Beagle and Mr. Hyde
Fly, You Stupid Kite, Fly!
How Long, Great Pumpkin, How Long?
It's Great to Be a Superstar
Kiss Her, You Blockhead!
My Anxieties Have Anxieties
Speak Softly, and Carry a Beagle
There Goes the Shutout
Summers Fly, Winters Walk
Thank Goodness for People
The Beagle Has Landed
What Makes You Think You're Happy?
And a Woodstock in a Birch Tree
A Smile Makes a Lousy Umbrella
The Mad Punter Strikes Again
There's a Vulture Outside
Here Comes the April Fool!
What Makes Musicians So Sarcastic?
A Kiss on the Nose Turns Anger Aside
It's Hard Work Being Bitter
I'm Not Your Sweet Babboo!
Stop Snowing on My Secretary
Always Stick Up for the Underbird
What's Wrong with Being Crabby?
Don't Hassle Me with Your Sighs, Chuck
The Way of the Fussbudget Is Not Easy
You're Weird, Sir!
It's a Long Way to Tipperary
Who's the Funny-Looking Kid with the Big Nose?
Sunday's Fun Day, Charlie Brown
You're Out of Your Mind, Charlie Brown!
You're the Guest of Honor, Charlie Brown
You Can't Win, Charlie Brown
Peanuts Every Sunday
The Unsinkable Charlie Brown
Good Grief, More Peanuts
You've Come a Long Way, Charlie Brown
The Cheshire Beagle
Duck, Here Comes Another Day!
Sarcasm Does Not Become You, Ma'am
Nothing Echoes Like an Empty Mailbox
I Heard A D Minus Call Me

HERE COMES THE APRIL FOOL!

by Charles M. Schulz

An Owl Book
Henry Holt and Company/New York

Henry Holt and Company, Inc.
Publishers since 1866
115 West 18th Street
New York, New York 10011

Henry Holt® is a registered trademark
of Henry Holt and Company, Inc.

Library of Congress Catalog Card Number: 92-53060

ISBN 0-8050-2058-6

Henry Holt books are available for special promotions
and premiums. For details contact: Director, Special Markets.

Originally published in 1980 by Holt, Rinehart and Winston in an
expanded editions as *Here Comes the April Fool!,* and included
strips from 1980.

New Owl Book Edition—1992

Printed in the United States of America
All first editions are printed on acid-free paper.∞

3   5   7   9   10   8   6   4   2

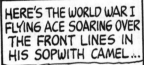

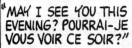

"GOOD EVENING, MISS...
BONSOIR, MADEMOISELLE"

"MAY I INVITE YOU TO
DANCE? PUIS-JE VOUS
INVITER À DANSER?
YOU DANCE VERY WELL..
VOUS DANSEZ TRÈS BIEN"

BONSOIR, MONSIEUR

RATS! I SWALLOWED
MY PHRASE BOOK!

HERE'S THE WORLD WAR I
FLYING ACE SITTING IN A
LITTLE CAFE...ONCE AGAIN
HE IS DEPRESSED...

HIS LEAVE IS OVER,
AND HE HAS FAILED
TO MEET THE CHARMING
FRENCH LASS...

HE DECIDES TO FORGET
HER BY DRINKING ROOT
BEER...GARÇON! ANOTHER
ROUND, S'IL VOUS PLAÎT!

UNFORTUNATELY, IT'S VERY
HARD TO FORGET ANYONE
BY DRINKING ROOT BEER!

HERE'S THE WORLD WAR I FLYING ACE DOWN BEHIND ENEMY LINES...

I CAN ALWAYS TELL WHEN I'M NEAR THE ENEMY...

GET OUT OF THE WAY, YOU STUPID BEAGLE!

THEY'RE NOT AS POLITE...

HERE'S THE WORLD WAR I FLYING ACE DOWN BEHIND ENEMY LINES WEARING ONE OF HIS FAMOUS DISGUISES

C MINUS ?!!

I WORK ALL NIGHT ON A PAPER, AND ALL I GET IS A "C MINUS"!

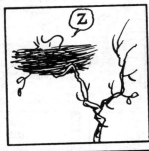

"HOW MANY ANGELS CAN STAND ON THE HEAD OF A PIN?"

THIS MUST BE KIND OF A PHILOSOPHICAL QUESTION, HUH, MA'AM?

THE HEAD OF A PIN, HUH? BOY, THAT'S A HARD ONE...

HOW ABOUT A PAPER CLIP?

GET THIS, CHUCK...SHE ASKS US HOW MANY ANGELS CAN STAND ON THE HEAD OF A PIN!

WHAT KIND OF A QUESTION IS THAT, CHUCK? HOW CAN YOU ANSWER SOMETHING LIKE THAT?

YOU CAN'T, PATTY...IT'S AN OLD THEOLOGICAL PROBLEM...THERE REALLY IS NO ANSWER...

THAT'S TOO BAD... I PUT DOWN, "EIGHT, IF THEY'RE SKINNY, AND FOUR IF THEY'RE FAT!"

YOU CAN'T SAY HOW MANY ANGELS CAN STAND ON THE HEAD OF A PIN, SIR... THERE IS NO ANSWER!

WELL, THAT'S JUST GREAT, MARCIE! IF I TRY TO ANSWER A QUESTION, I'M WRONG!

IF I DON'T ANSWER A QUESTION, I'M RIGHT!

THAT'S EDUCATION, SIR!

SORRY ABOUT MY MATH PAPER, MA'AM

ON MY WAY TO SCHOOL THIS MORNING, I SORT OF DROPPED IT IN THE MUD

MAYBE YOU CAN KIND OF BRUSH IT OFF A BIT WITH YOUR SLEEVE... WANNA TRY IT?

I GUESS NOT

INSCRUTABLE?

NO, MA'AM... I CAN'T SPELL INSCRUTABLE

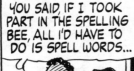

YOU SAID, IF I TOOK PART IN THE SPELLING BEE, ALL I'D HAVE TO DO IS SPELL WORDS...

YOU DIDN'T SAY I HAD TO SPELL 'EM RIGHT!

I WAS RUNNER-UP IN THE SPELLING BEE! HOW ABOUT THAT?

YOU WEREN'T RUNNER-UP, FRANKLIN...

YOU CAME IN SIXTEENTH...

I WAS RUNNER-UP TO THE KID WHO CAME IN FIFTEENTH!

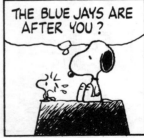

THE BLUE JAYS ARE AFTER YOU?

THEN YOU NEED ONE OF MY FAMOUS QUICK DISGUISES...

THERE! NOW THEY'LL THINK YOU'RE A RACCOON!

I WONDER WHAT TIME IT IS...

IT MUST BE LATE

THE MOON IS UP...

AND THE RACCOONS ARE OUT!

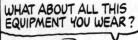

"THIS REPORTER HAS NEVER INTERVIEWED A WORSE BASEBALL TEAM"

"THE MANAGER IS INEPT AND THE PLAYERS ARE HOPELESS"

"WE WILL SAY, HOWEVER, THAT THE CATCHER IS KIND OF CUTE, AND THE RIGHT FIELDER, WHO HAS DARK HAIR, IS VERY BEAUTIFUL"

GOOD ARTICLE, HUH?

POW!

NOW I KNOW WHY WE PLAY BASEBALL IN THE SUMMER...

WHEN YOUR SHOES AND SOCKS GET KNOCKED OFF BY A LINE DRIVE, YOUR FEET DON'T GET COLD!

THAT WAS SOME LINE DRIVE, CHARLIE BROWN... IT KNOCKED YOUR SHOESIES AND YOUR SOCKIES RIGHT OFF!

MAYBE WE SHOULD COUNT TO SEE IF YOU STILL HAVE ALL YOUR TOESIES...

GET OUT OF HERE!

JUST FOR THAT, HE CAN COUNT HIS OWN TOESIES!

BONK!

THAT'S FORTY-NINE FLY BALLS IN A ROW!

HOW COULD ANYONE DROP FORTY-NINE FLY BALLS IN A ROW?

THE SUN GOT IN MY EYES FORTY-NINE TIMES!

NOW WHAT ARE YOU DOING?

I CAN SEE BETTER HERE

GET OUT THERE IN RIGHT FIELD, AND TRY TO CATCH THE BALL!

AND I DON'T WANT TO HEAR ANY EXCUSES TODAY!

DON'T TRY TO TELL ME THAT THE SUN GOT IN YOUR EYES! OR THE MOON, EITHER! OR THE CLOUDS, OR THE SMOG OR THE CRAB GRASS!

I DON'T WANT TO HEAR ABOUT THE GROUND MOVING, OR YOUR GLOVE BENDING OR YOUR SHOES COMING LOOSE! ALL I WANT TO HEAR IS THAT YOU CAUGHT THE BALL!

PLUNK

ACTUALLY, I WAS KIND OF LOOKING FORWARD TO A NEW EXCUSE...

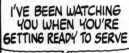

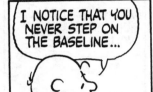

IT'S YOUR TURN.. ROLL THE DICE!

WHAT IF ROLLING THESE DICE LEADS ME TO A LIFE OF GAMBLING?

WHAT IF I CAN'T STOP? WHAT IF I BECOME A COMPULSIVE GAMBLER? WHAT IF I...

ROLLING DICE CAN RUIN YOU...SO CAN **NOT** ROLLING DICE!

THERE....I MOVED FIVE SQUARES..NOW, IT'S YOUR TURN...ROLL THE DICE!

IN THE TWENTY-EIGHTH CHAPTER OF EXODUS, IT TELLS OF 'URIM AND THUMMIM'.. SOME SCHOLARS SAY THESE WERE SMALL STONES LIKE DICE

THESE DICE WERE USED TO OBTAIN THE WILL OF GOD WHEN DECISIONS HAD TO BE MADE, AND...

ROLL THE DICE!

THAT'S A GOOD DECISION

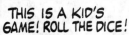

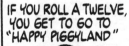

LET ME SEE THAT BOOK! WHAT IS IT?

PHOOEY! I WOULDN'T READ THIS FOR ANYTHING!

NOT IN A MILLION YEARS! FORGET IT! NO WAY!!

LUCY HAS NO TROUBLE JUDGING A BOOK BY ITS COVER!

THE YEARS ARE GOING BY FAST

WILL YOU LOVE ME WHEN I'M OLD AND GRAY?

IF I DON'T LOVE YOU NOW, WHY SHOULD I LOVE YOU THEN?

BECAUSE I'LL BE A SWEET OLD LADY!

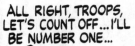

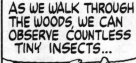

A HIKE THROUGH THE WOODS IN THE SPRING CAN BE A JOY AND AN INSPIRATION...

?

IT CAN REVIVE YOUR SPIRITS, AND IT CAN..

.. GET YOU INTO MORE TROUBLE THAN YOU EVER DREAMED OF IN YOUR WHOLE STUPID LIFE!

FINE BUNCH OF BEAGLE SCOUTS YOU GUYS ARE!

YOU SPOT FOUR CHICKS, AND YOU RUN OFF AND LEAVE ME!

YOU ALL FORGOT YOUR BEAGLE SCOUT OATH, "DON'T CUT OUT ON A FRIEND"

INCIDENTALLY, DID YOU HAVE A GOOD TIME?

RING!

HELLO? OH, HI! NO, NOTHING MUCH...

JUST SITTING HERE WATCHING THE LOWER HALF OF A MOVIE!

A GROCERY CLERK?

SURE, WHY NOT?

BUT WHAT MAKES YOU THINK YOU COULD BE A GROCERY CLERK?

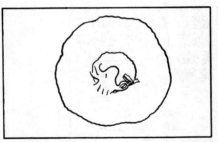

WHAT ARE YOU DOING HERE? YOU'RE SUPPOSED TO BE OUT SOMEWHERE SITTING ON A BRANCH CHIRPING

THAT'S YOUR JOB...PEOPLE EXPECT TO HEAR BIRDS CHIRPING WHEN THEY WAKE UP IN THE MORNING...

CHIRP!

YOU ONLY CHIRPED ONCE...YOU CAN'T BRIGHTEN SOMEONE'S DAY WITH ONE CHIRP!

CHIRP CHIRP CHIRP CHIRP CHIRP CHIRP

THERE, NOW! DIDN'T THAT GIVE YOU A FEELING OF REAL SATISFACTION?

THE BAD NEWS IS YOU'RE SUPPOSED TO DO THAT EVERY MORNING FOR THE REST OF YOUR LIFE!

KLUNK

HOW CAN I DO A REPORT ON HANNIBAL, MARCIE? I'VE NEVER HEARD OF HIM!

RUN DOWN TO THE LIBRARY, SIR, AND LOOK HIM UP IN THE ENCYCLOPEDIA... THAT'S WHAT I DID..

MAYBE IT'LL SNOW TOMORROW, AND ALL THE SCHOOLS WILL BE CLOSED..

GOOD NIGHT, SIR!

This is my report. Here it is.

What follows is my report.

Yes, this is my report.

So far it isn't much, is it?

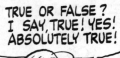

WHEN WE GET TO HIGH SCHOOL, I'M HOPING THAT WE'LL HAVE LOCKERS NEXT TO EACH OTHER

THAT WOULD BE AN ODD COMBINATION! HA HA HA HA HA!!

GET IT? LOCKERS HAVE COMBINATION LOCKS! AN ODD COMBINATION! GET IT?

MUSICIANS SHOULD NEVER TRY TO BE FUNNY

YOU NEVER CALL ME "HONEY BUTTER"

IF YOU CALLED ME "HONEY BUTTER," I'D PROBABLY TINGLE ALL OVER...

FORGET IT

SO MUCH FOR TINGLING!

WHERE'S LUCY?

SHE'S LYING IN HER BEAN BAG SULKING

THEN I WON'T BOTHER HER...

I KNOW BETTER THAN TO DISTURB A GOOD SULK

SMART

WHO IS THAT?

THAT'S BLACKJACK SNOOPY, THE WORLD FAMOUS RIVER BOAT GAMBLER...

IS HE FAMOUS BECAUSE HE'S SUCH A GOOD CARD PLAYER?

NO, BECAUSE I HAVE TWO MUSTACHES!

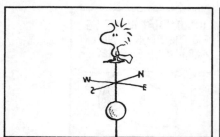

YOU LOOK EXHAUSTED! RUNNING A FARM IS HARD WORK

WELL, OKAY...

I DON'T MIND HELPING OUT ON A FRIEND'S FARM ONCE IN A WHILE...

BUT I HATE BEING THE SCARECROW!

I'VE BEEN THINKING... YOU HAD SUCH GOOD LUCK RAISING AND SELLING YOUR RADISH...

MAYBE YOU SHOULD GO FOR THE BIG MONEY...

YES, THAT'S WHAT YOU SHOULD DO...

TRY TO RAISE A SOYBEAN!

THERE'S SOMEONE HERE FROM THE COUNTY TO SEE YOU...

IT'S ABOUT YOUR GARDEN.. I THINK THE FARMER NEXT DOOR CLAIMS YOU'RE USING PART OF HIS LAND

THAT'S RIDICULOUS!! WHAT DOES THIS GUY FROM THE COUNTY LOOK LIKE ANYWAY?

WHO IN THE WORLD IS THIS GUY?

THIS IS THE COUNTY SURVEYOR..HE'S TRYING TO FIND THE PROPERTY LINE BETWEEN YOUR GARDEN AND THE FARMER...

FARMER? WHAT FARMER?

N 27°

BEEP!

HERE'S THE WORLD FAMOUS SURVEYOR PREPARING A LAND DESCRIPTION...

" RICHARD ROE... N 81° 02' W 184.32 ft. S 61° 47' W 187.15 ft. "

" JOHN DOE...HMM.... N 19° 45' W 285.62 ft. "

EXCUSE ME..I THINK YOU'RE STANDING ON MAIN STREET

HERE'S THE WORLD WAR I FLYING ACE IN FRANCE...

BONJOUR, MONSIEUR... JE SUIS EN PANNE

OÙ EST LE GARAGE LE PLUS PROCHE?

I FALL IN LOVE WITH ANYONE WHO WILL TALK TO ME

HERE'S THE WORLD WAR I FLYING ACE IN PARIS...

HE IS SITTING IN A SMALL SIDEWALK CAFE WITH A BEAUTIFUL YOUNG FRENCH LASS...

HE MUST IMPRESS HER WITH HIS SOPHISTICATED MANNER

MAY I SEE THE ROOT BEER LIST, PLEASE?

HERE'S THE WORLD WAR I FLYING ACE TAKING A BEAUTIFUL FRENCH LASS OUT TO DINNER...

POTAGE AU CERFEUIL... CANARD A L'ORANGE...

ESCARGOTS... FONDS D'ARTICHAUT... PÂTE DE FOIE GRAS... ET BEIGNETS, S'IL VOUS PLAÎT

UN ROOT BEER, S'IL VOUS PLAÎT

HERE'S THE WORLD WAR I FLYING ACE SAYING GOODBYE TO THE BEAUTIFUL FRENCH LASS BEFORE HE RETURNS TO THE FRONT...

SNIF!

NICE

QUICKLY HE SEARCHES THROUGH HIS PHRASE BOOK FOR THE WORDS THAT WILL EXPRESS WHAT IS IN HIS HEART...

RATS!

HELLO, SALLY? I JUST CALLED TO FIND OUT HOW YOUR BROTHER IS...

I SUPPOSE YOU THOUGHT I'D THINK YOU WERE CALLING TO ASK ME TO GO TO THE MOVIES!

WELL, I DIDN'T!! AND I WOULDN'T GO TO THE MOVIES WITH YOU NOW EVEN IF YOU ASKED ME, SO THERE!

WELL, HOW IS HE?

HOW IS WHO?

HOSPITAL ZONE QUIET!

EMERGENCY ENTRANCE

GOOD AFTERNOON, MA'AM! I DON'T MEAN TO BE ANY TROUBLE...

BUT I HAVE THE AWFUL FEELING THAT I MAY BE AN EMERGENCY!

I SAW THE SIGN THAT SAYS "EMERGENCY ENTRANCE" SO I CAME IN...

I DON'T FEEL GOOD...I FEEL KIND OF WOOZY..

NO, MY MOM AND DAD ARE AT THE BARBERS' PICNIC SO IT WOULDN'T DO ME ANY GOOD TO GO HOME...

NO, MA'AM..I DIDN'T GET HIT ON THE HEAD WITH A FLY BALL

HEY, SALLY, THIS IS PEPPERMINT PATTY...LET ME TALK TO CHUCK...

I DON'T KNOW WHERE HE IS...SOMEBODY SAID HE GOT SICK AT THE BALL GAME, BUT HE NEVER CAME HOME..

ANYWAY, I'M TOO BUSY TO TALK RIGHT NOW...

I'M MOVING MY THINGS INTO HIS ROOM...

YES, MA'AM...THAT'S MY PRESENT ADDRESS... MY NAME IS CHARLES BROWN.. I'M EIGHT AND A HALF...

YES, I'VE HAD ALL MY SHOTS..NO, MA'AM, NO ALLERGIES..INSURANCE?

I SUPPOSE SO...NO, I DON'T HAVE A SOCIAL SECURITY NUMBER...

SPEAKING OF MONEY, HOW'S YOUR FUND RAISING PROGRAM COMING ALONG?

NO, THIS IS SALLY... I'M HIS SISTER... HE'S WHERE?

IT'S THE "ACE MEMORIAL HOSPITAL"...YOUR OWNER'S IN THE HOSPITAL!

NO, MY PARENTS ARE AT THE BARBERS' PICNIC...YES, I'LL TELL THEM..HOW LONG WILL HE BE IN THE HOSPITAL? IS HE GOING TO GET WELL?

SHOULD I FEED THE DOG?

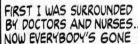

Dear Big Brother, I hope you are feeling better.

Things are fine here at home. I have moved into your room.

Don't worry about your personal things.

The flea market was a success.

I'M SO WORRIED ABOUT POOR CHARLIE BROWN LYING THERE IN THE HOSPITAL...

HE'S GOT TO GET WELL! HE'S GOT TO! OH, BOO HOO HOO HOO! SOB!

IT'S INTERESTING THAT YOU SHOULD CRY OVER HIM WHEN YOU'RE THE ONE WHO ALWAYS TREATED HIM SO MEAN!

AND STOP WIPING YOUR TEARS WITH MY PIANO!

WE CAN'T VISIT CHUCK BECAUSE WE'RE TOO YOUNG? RATS!

JUST FOR THAT WE'LL GO ACROSS THE STREET AND SIT ON A PARK BENCH AND STARE UP AT HIS ROOM!

IT'S A WELL-KNOWN FACT, MARCIE, THAT A PATIENT WILL RECOVER FASTER IF HE KNOWS A FRIEND IS STARING UP AT HIS ROOM...

YOU SHOULD HAVE BEEN A DOCTOR, SIR

THE LIGHT IN CHUCK'S ROOM JUST WENT OUT, MARCIE

HE'S PROBABLY GONE TO SLEEP, SIR

SLEEP WELL, CHUCK!

HOPE YOU FEEL BETTER IN THE MORNING!

WE MISS YOU, CHUCK!

WE LOVE YOU, CHUCK!

WE DO?

WE DO CHUCK'!!

YOUR OWNER'S STILL IN THE HOSPITAL SO I GUESS I HAVE TO FEED YOU

IF I CUT MY FINGER ON THE CAN OPENER, I'M GONNA SUE YOU!

WHO CARES?

A CASE LIKE THAT COULD DRAG ON FOR YEARS

I'M SO WORRIED ABOUT CHARLIE BROWN, I CAN'T EAT OR SLEEP...

WELL, IF YOU GET SICK, TOO, THAT SURE WON'T HELP HIM...

MAYBE IF HE THOUGHT HE WAS MAKING ME SICK, HE'D GET BETTER

MAYBE I COULD SEND HIM A THREATENING LETTER

CHARLIE BROWN, I KNOW YOU CAN'T HEAR ME, BUT I WANT TO MAKE YOU A PROMISE...

IF YOU GET WELL, I PROMISE I'LL NEVER PULL THE FOOTBALL AWAY AGAIN!

THAT'S QUITE A PROMISE

I'LL BET HE FEELS BETTER ALREADY!

LET ME GET THIS STRAIGHT

IF CHARLIE BROWN GETS WELL, YOU PROMISE NEVER TO PULL THE FOOTBALL AWAY AGAIN?

THAT IS MY SOLEMN PROMISE!

HE'S SURE TO GET WELL NOW.. HE HAS SOMETHING TO LIVE FOR!

IF YOU SIT ON A PARK BENCH ACROSS FROM THE HOSPITAL AND STARE UP AT HIS WINDOW, THE PATIENT GETS BETTER...

POOR CHUCK..I HATE TO THINK OF HIM LYING UP THERE IN THAT HOSPITAL ROOM

YOU KIND OF LIKE CHUCK, DON'T YOU, SIR?

WELL, I..YOU KNOW... I FEEL SORT OF..YOU KNOW...HE..I..HE..

I LOVE CHUCK! I THINK HE'S REAL NEAT!

REAL NEAT? YOU THINK HE'S REAL NEAT?

I SURE DO! SOMEDAY I HOPE HE'LL ASK ME TO THE SENIOR PROM!

IN FACT, IF HE ASKED ME, I'D EVEN MARRY CHUCK!

COME WITH ME, MARCIE

IS THIS THE EMERGENCY ENTRANCE, MA'AM? WE'RE FRIENDS OF CHARLES BROWN

I HAVE ANOTHER PATIENT FOR YOU.. I THINK SHE'S SICKER THAN HE IS!

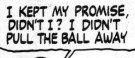

WE MUST NEVER FORGET THAT WE ARE SURROUNDED BY POTENTIAL ENEMIES...

I THINK WE SHOULD PRACTICE SOME DRILLS TO SEE HOW YOU REACT IN AN EMERGENCY...

BE READY, NOW... I'M GOING TO TRY TO CATCH YOU BY SURPRISE...

BEAR!

VERY GOOD! EXCELLENT REACTION!

SNAKE!

GOOD! QUICK MOVE!

BE READY.... BE ALERT...

CHICKEN HAWK!

WELL, THAT LAST ONE MAY NEED A LITTLE WORK..

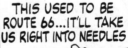

"NEEDLES, CALIFORNIA.. A RECREATIONAL CENTER ON THE COLORADO RIVER"

"ELEVATION, 463 FEET... AVERAGE RAINFALL, FIVE INCHES PER YEAR..."

"ATTRACTIONS IN THE AREA ARE OLD GHOST TOWNS AND TOPOCK SWAMP"

THAT MUST BE WHERE MY BROTHER SPIKE LIVES...TOPOCK SWAMP!

SPIKE!

WOOF!

MY BROTHER SPIKE! WOW! IT'S GOOD TO SEE YOU AGAIN!

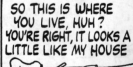
SO THIS IS WHERE YOU LIVE, HUH? YOU'RE RIGHT, IT LOOKS A LITTLE LIKE MY HOUSE

I'M GLAD OUR MOM NEVER SAW THIS

SPIKE, YOU LOOK TERRIBLE...WHAT'S HAPPENED TO YOU?

MOM AND DAD DIDN'T RAISE YOU TO BE A DESERT RAT...YOU'RE WASTING YOUR LIFE...

IT'S NOT TOO LATE TO MAKE SOMETHING OF YOURSELF... COME HOME WITH ME..I'LL HELP YOU... WHAT DO YOU SAY?

SNIF

SCHULZ

WHY DO YOU WANT TO LIVE OUT HERE IN THE DESERT WITH THE SNAKES, AND THE LIZARDS AND THE COYOTES?

COME HOME WITH ME, SPIKE, AND LIVE A NORMAL LIFE...

OH, REALLY? WELL, I CAN UNDERSTAND THAT..

IT'S HARD TO LEAVE WHEN YOUR BOWLING TEAM IS IN FIRST PLACE...

SCHULZ

EVERYONE IS COMPLAINING ABOUT THE HEAT, CHARLIE BROWN...

I KNOW... I HAVE TO ADMIT IT'S PRETTY WARM FOR PLAYING BASEBALL

THE ONLY ONE WHO HASN'T COMPLAINED IS LUCY...

SCHULZ

NEXT YEAR I'M GONNA BE A FREE AGENT

YOU ARE, HUH?

DO YOU KNOW WHAT A FREE AGENT IS?

NOPE

BUT I'M GONNA BE ONE!!

SCHULZ

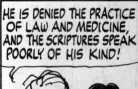

Z

Z

REPEAT THE QUESTION, WILL YOU, MA'AM? THERE'S AN ECHO DOWN HERE...

I'VE GOT IT!

YES, MA'AM, I THINK I KNOW THE ANSWER

SIXTEEN..FOUR.. THIRTY-SEVEN

ON SECOND THOUGHT, THAT MAY BE MY LOCKER COMBINATION!